Los Angeles

★ GREAT ★ CITIES ★ OF THE ★ USA ★

☆ ☆ ☆

LIBRARY OF CONGRESS CATALOGING-IN-PUBLICATION DATA

Stewart, Gail, 1949-
    Los Angeles / by Gail B. Stewart.
      p. cm. -- (Great Cities of the United States)
    Summary: An introduction to the history, economy, people, and notable sites of the
second largest city in the United States.
    ISBN 0-86592-540-2
    1. Los Angeles (Calif.)--Description--1981- --Guide-books--Juvenile literature.
[1. Los Angeles (Calif.)--Description--Guides.] I. Title. II. Series: Stewart, Gail,
1949-   Great Cities of the United States.
    F869.L83S74 1989
    917.94'940453--dc20   89-32407
                                                         CIP
                                                           AC

☆ ☆ ☆

Los Angeles

★ GREAT ★ CITIES ★ OF THE ★ USA ★

TEXT BY
GAIL STEWART

DESIGN & PRODUCTION BY
MARK E. AHLSTROM
(The Bookworks)

**ROURKE
ENTERPRISES,
INC.**
Vero Beach, FL 32964
U.S.A.

City of
Displaced Persons...

☆ ☆ ☆

TABLE OF CONTENTS

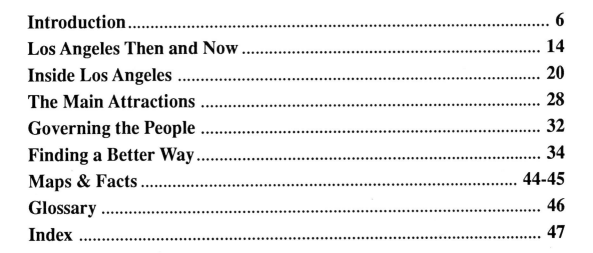

CREDITS

All photos: FPG International

J. Randkler .... cover photo, 4
J. Blank 7, 42-43
Peter Beney 8
David Bartruff 10
P.K. 11
R. Mackson 12-13
Leverett Bradley 17
Travelpix 18
Philip Wallick 19

Suzanne Murphy 21
J. Chen 22
Peter Gridley 25, 31
Marvin J. Wolf 26, 32, 36-37, 40, 41
H. DeCruyenaere 30
Jim Pickerell 35
J. Scowen 39

TYPESETTING AND LAYOUT: THE FINAL WORD
PRINTING: WORZALLA PUBLISHING CO.

☆ ☆ ☆

City of Displaced Persons

For many years city officials of Los Angeles have hoped that someone would write a beautiful ballad about their city. They thought how lucky San Francisco was to have the famous song "I Left My Heart in San Francisco." Chicago has "My Kind of Town," and New York has handfuls of songs—even ones about individual streets!

But Los Angeles had no truly memorable song that people could hum. There was no romantic ballad about Sunset Boulevard or Beverly Hills. There didn't seem to be a song that could make ex-Angelenos (a person from Los Angeles is an Angeleno) homesick for their city.

It can't be that Los Angeles isn't big enough to rate its own song. On the contrary, in the mid-1980's it officially passed Chicago as the second largest city in the country. L.A., as Los Angeles is commonly called, is huge—both in terms of population (about 7.5 million in the metro area) and in area (about 460 square miles). So with so much of it, why no song?

Finally someone came up with a possible explanation for Los Angeles' lack of a song.

"This place is not a ballad town," explained one Los Angeles musician. "Ballads are slow and lovely. Los Angeles is hip, it's fun, it's busy, and it's big. But even L.A.'s biggest fans wouldn't call it lovely."

"And besides," he went on, "it's impossible to make ex-Angelenos homesick for the place, since there are no ex-Angelenos. Everybody that comes here stays!"

Most Angelenos would agree. Their city is not perfect, they know. However, it has a strange magic about it that makes visitors want to stay.

Part of L.A.'s magic is its cli-

Wilshire Boulevard leads from the Pacific Ocean to downtown Los Angeles.

The Los Angeles climate is comfortable all year.

mate. It is usually sunny and comfortably warm. In the summer the average temperature is about 75 degrees (F); in the winter it's usually around 65. In early spring when people in places like Minnesota and Illinois are still shivering with cold, Angelenos are flocking to the beaches. And does L.A. have beaches—over 80 miles of them!

The climate of Los Angeles is apparent by the types of homes that are built in the city. Almost every house has a deck or patio. Many even have backyard swimming pools!

Another part of L.A.'s magic is its reputation as the center of the entertainment industry. For many years Los Angeles—especially a part of it called Hollywood—has been the place where most movies and television shows are filmed. Quite a few visitors to L.A., in fact, make it a point to visit one of the film studios, or the NBC Studios in nearby Burbank. It is in "Beautiful Downtown Burbank" that the Johnny Carson show has been filmed for many years. Others who come to Los Angeles have dreams of being "discovered" by a Hollywood producer and becoming actors. Many more just dream of catching a glimpse of their favorite movie star in a restaurant or shop.

The West Coast, and L.A. in particular, has always been known as a place where you can expect the offbeat, the unusual. Comedians make jokes about crazy California ideas and styles. In a sense, the jokes have some truth behind them. California, especially L.A., has become a magnet over the years, attracting those with new ideas. Many have come from the South, or the Midwest, or even the East Coast, because they might have felt that the free-and-easy lifestyle of L.A. was more suitable for them.

Many have come with almost a pioneer spirit, hoping to change the style of America's clothing, or its music—you name it. Some of the new ideas might be brilliant, and some might be downright silly. But it's true—anything that's "hot" is likely to have originated in L.A.

Someone said about Los Angeles that one of the hardest things in the world was to find a native Angeleno—in other words, one who was born and raised there. Although this is somewhat of an exaggeration, it is true that Los Angeles is made up of lots of transplanted Northerners, Midwesterners, and Southerners—not to mention the hundreds of thousands of immigrants from other countries. More than half of the 7.5 million people in the L.A. metropolitan area have come from other places.

This "city of displaced persons" has even extended to L.A.'s exciting professional sports teams. The World Champion L.A. Dodgers of

In 1984, the Olympic Games were held at the Los Angeles Memorial Coliseum.

At the Summer Olympics in Los Angeles, July 28—August 12, 1984, the United States won 83 gold medals and finished first in unofficial team standings.

baseball's National League were once the Brooklyn Dodgers. The World Champion L.A. Lakers of the NBA were once Minneapolis' team. Both pro football teams in L.A. are transplants, too—the Rams from Cleveland and the Raiders from nearby Oakland. The L.A. Kings, the city's pro hockey team, almost started a border war when they lured superstar Wayne Gretzky from Edmonton, Canada!

The beautiful climate, the glamour of Hollywood, the lure of a job in one of the city's many industries, the easygoing way of life—all have lured newcomers to L.A. And in spite of the problems Los Angeles faces—everything from horrible poverty to violent gangs, earthquakes, and unbreathable air—most of the people who have visited have ended up staying.

The Los Angeles Memorial Coliseum, in Exposition Park, is the home of the Los Angeles Raiders football team.

The area that is now the city of Los Angeles was inhabited as far back as the 1500's. At that time a branch of the Shoshoni tribe of Native Americans lived there, in a village they called Yang-na. A Portuguese explorer happened upon Yang-na in 1542 and marked it on his map. However, it wasn't until 200 years later that any other explorers found the place.

Spanish Explorers and a Long Name

In 1769 a Spanish explorer named Gaspar de Portola, together with Juan Crespi, a priest, came upon the village. They were impressed with the beauty of the area, and its closeness to the sea. The mild temperatures and sunshine so pleased them, in fact, that Crespi wrote in his journal that the place had all that was needed for a good settlement.

Portola and Crespi gave the place a new name—*Nuestra Señora la Reina de Los Angeles de Porciuncula.* In English, that means "Our Lady the Queen of the Angels of Porciuncula." Porciuncula, by the way, was the name of a famous chapel in Italy, associated with Crespi's religion. The village's new long name was shortened quite a bit as time went on!

Within a couple of years, Spanish colonization of the area started. (It's important to understand that Spain then owned the land that is now Mexico.) Priests built a mission, or church, just east of what is now downtown Los Angeles, called San Gabriel Arcangel. The San Gabriel Mission was the first of 21 missions built by Spanish priests in the area of Southern California.

As the missions were completed, the next step in colonizing the area was to get a town started. The Spanish governor of California wanted to encourage people to settle in this new place. He pledged to send soldiers and lots of supplies to Los Angeles. The supplies would help the newcomers build a good strong town, and the soldiers' presence would make the settlers feel safe.

The first group of settlers that arrived in Los Angeles was made up of 11 men, 11 women, and 22 children. The group included Indians, Spaniards, blacks, and some of mixed backgrounds. Things went fairly smoothly for the little colony, and by the year 1800 there were more than 300 people living there. Mostly they were farmers and cattle ranchers.

☆ ☆ ☆

Los Angeles today has a population that is roughly 62 percent white; 17 percent black; 7 percent Asian and Pacific Islander; 1 percent American Indian, Eskimo, or Aleutian; and 13 percent not classified elsewhere. People of Hispanic origin (who may be of any race) make up about 27 percent of the total population.

From Mexican Control to American City

In 1821 Mexico won its independence from Spain and became a free country. All of California was then controlled by Mexico, not Spain. Los Angeles figured pretty importantly in the new scheme of things. It was for a time the capital of Mexican-owned California.

The first known American to arrive in Los Angeles was a fur trapper and trader named Jebediah Smith. He was the first of many Americans who would visit the area. The Mexicans weren't very happy about the arrival of so many Americans. They feared that the Americans wanted to have this land for themselves. They were probably right. As they pushed their way westward, many American settlers just assumed that whatever they found and liked, they could keep.

As more and more white Americans came to the Los Angeles area, tensions between Mexico and the

United States became very strong. War broke out in 1846. Mexico eventually lost this war, and signed a treaty giving the United States all rights to California.

Los Angeles continued to grow, but it was gaining a reputation as a lawless and violent town. It seemed to be a haven for criminals from all over the United States who were hiding out from the law. During the California Gold Rush of 1849, in fact, Los Angeles was often called *Los Diablos* (Spanish for "The Devils.")

By the middle of the 19th century, Los Angeles was incorporated as a city. It had a population of 1,610. A few months after it officially became a city, California was admitted as a state, and the population began to increase rapidly.

Los Angeles Takes Off

There were several reasons for the surge in Los Angeles' population. One of the most important was the connection of Los Angeles to San Francisco by railroad. Soon after, other railroad connections were made to cities in the East.

Some of the railroads had fare "wars"—each trying to outdo the other. As a result, in 1886 it cost only a dollar to travel from Chicago to Los Angeles! Many people who had heard about the beautiful City of the Angels on California's west coast could afford to visit. Most were so impressed that they decided to stay.

The 1890's brought a new flood of visitors, for oil was discovered in the area. People were buying land, hoping to find oil on their property so that they would become rich. By the year 1900 the population of L.A. was 100,000.

Los Angeles became even more important in 1914. It built an artificial harbor in nearby San Pedro Bay. In addition to the farming and ranching industries, the city now could compete as a center of trade. Being an important seaport—the most important on the West Coast, in fact—was an important factor in attracting even more people to the city. A harbor meant lots of new jobs,

Los Angeles harbor, built in 1914 at San Pedro, contributed to the city's growth.

and there were people eager to fill them.

The 1920's brought the rise of two key industries. The first was the motion picture industry. All of the important studios were located in Los Angeles. The second industry was the building of aircraft. After World War I many airplane factories opened up in the L.A. area, and that resulted in a huge number of jobs. By 1930 Los Angeles' population had jumped to more than 1.2 million.

World War II was even better for the economy of Los Angeles. Aircraft plants like North American, Lockheed, and Douglas were important to the country's war effort, and production was stepped up to meet the demand for bigger and better aircraft. It was during this period that many blacks from the East and Midwest came to Los Angeles. Many of them got jobs in the aircraft-re-

Paramount Studio was one of many that made Los Angeles an entertainment center. The motion picture industry began in the 1920's.

lated plants in the city.

As Los Angeles grew in population, it desperately needed to grow in area, as well. All these new people needed places to live, and the city didn't have any more room. Los Angeles began to annex small towns and villages around the city into a bigger metro area. It is because of this "horizontal growth" that Los Angeles has been called "100 Suburbs in Search of a City."

The sprawling metropolis of Los Angeles has sometimes been called "100 Suburbs in Search of a City."

INSIDE LOS ANGELES

Because of the sprawling nature of the city, Los Angeles tends to rely less on its downtown area. In other cities such as Houston or Chicago, the downtown is the hub of shopping, business, and finance. But in L.A. there are interesting things going on in all sections of the city, and for that reason, visitors often leave L.A. not sure if they've even seen downtown!

Downtown L.A.

It may not be the center of Los Angeles' activity, but there are interesting things to see downtown. The Los Angeles City Hall is a distinctive landmark in the downtown area. For a long time, City Hall was the tallest building in L.A., at 32 stories high. After it was built, a law was passed forbidding the building of structures more than 15 stories high, because of the danger of earthquakes.

For many years, City Hall was the one exception, and it stood out among all the shorter buildings.

In 1957, however, the law was repealed. Newer, more modern building methods enabled engineers to create safer tall buildings. City Hall is no longer the tallest building in the city, but it continues to impress visitors with its beautiful white tower and the elaborate mosaics inside.

Another interesting part of the downtown section of L.A. is the site of the original city, called Pueblo de Los Angeles, or "City of the Angels." Here is Olvera Street, the city's oldest street, and the Old Plaza, or market square. This area has been restored so that it looks just as it did 200 years ago when it was a Mexican village. There are sidewalk vendors and wonderful things to eat. Cars are not allowed in this section of the city.

There are a few residential areas

City Hall, in the heart of the downtown area, is a 32-story landmark.

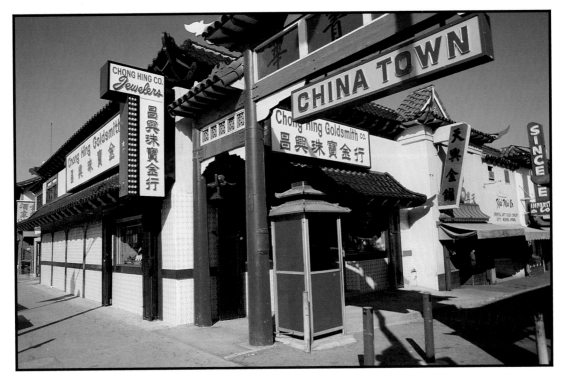

L.A.'s Chinatown has a culture all its own.

in the downtown area. One is Chinatown, which lies north of Pueblo de Los Angeles. Chinatown has many interesting shops and businesses. Many of the residents of Chinatown don't speak any English at all, and rarely leave the area. Many of the Chinese in Chinatown wear native dress. Visitors sometimes have to remind themselves that they are actually in Southern California and not Beijing!

Little Tokyo is another ethnic community, lying on the eastern border of the downtown area. Because of the heavy trade between the United States and Japan, and because the Port of Los Angeles handles much of the shipping trade with Japan, it's no wonder that there are many Japanese who make their home in L.A. There are many examples of Japanese culture in Little Tokyo—colorful toy shops, wonderful food stores and restaurants, and even a Japanese version of a Shakey's Pizza Parlor!

South Central Los Angeles

The part of Los Angeles known as the South Central area is almost entirely black. It is probably the largest black community in the United States. While some of the South Central area is made up of nice houses on tree-lined streets, most of it is poor and run-down.

During World War II there were many jobs opening up in the aircraft factories and other plants that contributed to the war. It was during this time of high opportunity that many black families moved to Los Angeles, hoping to find good jobs and a better way of life.

However, due to a number of factors—from overcrowding to poor education—the black community has remained largely a poor one. The South Central part of L.A. includes an area called Watts, which lies about 8 miles directly south of downtown.

It was in Watts that 34 people died in a riot in 1965. Protesting poor living conditions and other kinds of unequal treatment, blacks in Watts destroyed many millions of dollars worth of property. More than 1,000 people were injured in the rioting, looting, and burning, which lasted for six days.

Today there are still problems in this area of L.A. The issues which troubled the community in 1965 have not been resolved. Unemployment is high, education is not good, crime is violent, and drugs are everywhere. Angelenos are not at all proud of South Central L.A., and no one has any easy answer to the problems.

Central L.A./ Hollywood

Central L.A. is made up almost entirely of the community called Hollywood. Hollywood is famous for the many movie and television stars that work in this area of L.A. Many of the large movie studios are located in Central Los Angeles.

Two of the most famous streets in

the country are found in this part of L.A.—Hollywood Boulevard and Sunset Boulevard. The first, Hollywood Boulevard, is renowned for its Walk of Fame. The Walk of Fame consists of more than 2,500 black and orange stars that glitter in the sidewalk along Hollywood Boulevard. Each star is engraved with the name of a Hollywood movie star who has achieved greatness.

Sunset Boulevard winds its way for 25 miles through Los Angeles all the way to the Pacific Coast. In Central L.A. it is called the Sunset Strip, or just "The Strip." The Strip is well-known for its exciting nightspots and shops. Many people claim to have run into movie stars along the Strip at night.

In addition to the studios themselves, many of the businesses in Hollywood are movie-related. There are florists, for instance, who specialize in providing huge numbers of plants to studios. A movie might call for a jungle scene, or a garden. In cases like these, the florist would provide the "props." Other businesses which depend heavily on the movie industry are electrical contractors and lighting suppliers.

West L.A.

If Hollywood is where the stars work, then West L.A. is where many of them live. The community of Beverly Hills, located in West L.A., is famous for its glamorous residents. It is interesting to note that although L.A. has annexed many communities around it, Beverly Hills has remained independent.

Most visitors to L.A. insist on including a trip to Beverly Hills to see some of the most beautiful houses in the city. Many are owned by Hollywood stars, and almost all have big swimming pools or tennis courts. Some are hidden behind large walls, built to discourage overeager tourists and autograph-seekers. Part of the beauty of the Beverly Hills area is that it is remote. Much of the area is bordered by the Santa Monica Mountains, and the streets are hilly and curved.

There are three other very wealthy communities in the West L.A. area:

Many movie stars live in Beverly Hills.

Brentwood, Pacific Palisades, and Bel Air. Many movie and television personalities live there, as do many professional people.

The Westwood area of West L.A. is the location of the University of California at Los Angeles, or UCLA, as it is known. The school is huge! It is the largest of all the branches of the University of California. It is so big, in fact, that most students need cars to get from one class to another!

Century City is also a part of West L.A. Built on more than 180 acres of land that was once the location of 20th Century-Fox, Century City is a billion-dollar planned community. There are office buildings, apartment houses, a luxury hotel, many restaurants, and even a theater. All of the buildings in Century City are on what look like rollers built into the foundation. This makes it unlikely that an earthquake could damage the structure of the buildings and trap people inside.

The Valley

Although pretty boring in terms of architecture or history, the area of the San Fernando Valley, or "the Valley," as it is called, is home to more than one-third of all Angelenos. It is made up of shopping malls, freeways, and many housing

Century City, in West Los Angeles, was built on the former site of the 20th Century -Fox movie studio.

developments. Much of the pollution that plagues Los Angeles seems to settle in the Valley, trapped by calm air and the Santa Monica Mountains.

In the early 1980's, teenage "Valley Girls" took some good-natured ribbing from the media and other Angelenos about their strange slang. "Gag me with a spoon" and "to the max" are two of the famous Valley expressions.

East Los Angeles

Since the early part of the 20th century, the east part of L.A. has been the neighborhood of the working poor. Many of the first inhabitants of East L.A. were poor Jewish families. Now, however, the area is almost all Mexican-American, or "Chicano." The people there refer to their neighborhood as the *barrio*, which is Spanish for "neighborhood."

The barrio is home to more than 800,000 people. Most are very poor. A large number of the people there speak no English at all, which adds to their problems in finding jobs. It also makes it hard for the kids to do well in school.

Overcrowded conditions hamper those who are trying to improve the neighborhood. City officials say that the overcrowding in the barrio is due to the high number of illegals there. Illegals are people who have come into the United States illegally, crossing over the border from Mexico without permission. Most of these people have come to America to find work or a better way of life for their families. Unfortunately, most of the illegals are uneducated and unable to speak English, making their search for a better life difficult.

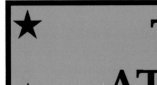

Concrete Souvenirs—the Chinese Theatre

One of the sights that continues to attract visitors to L.A. is Mann's (formerly Graumann's) Chinese Theatre. Built by Sid Graumann in 1927, it was supposed to reflect the wild, flamboyant atmosphere of Hollywood. Graumann had already built a huge theater in an Egyptian style of architecture, but he thought that the Chinese style might be really different.

The Chinese Theatre is a movie theater, but its fame has more to do with its courtyard outside than the shows inside. There are more than 150 sets of hand and footprints set in cement in the courtyard—belonging to Hollywood's most famous stars. It's always been an honor (and a photo opportunity) for a star to be asked to stand and sign his or her name in the cement. Roy Roger's horse Trigger has his hoof prints there, too, although we can assume someone else signed his name!

A Deadly Drink of Water— the Tar Pits

Located just east of the Beverly Hills area in Hancock Park, the La Brea Tar Pits are really an interesting place to visit. "La Brea," by the way, means "the tar." The tar pits are where many thousands of animals died in prehistoric times. Although they look like lakes, the tar pits actually have liquid tar, or asphalt, on the bottom. This tar was formed because tiny cracks in the earth's surface allowed natural gas and oil to seep into the lake bottom. Over many thousands of years, the bottom turned into black, syrupy tar.

Animals that lived 40,000 years ago, such as sabertooth tigers, mammoths, giant vultures, huge sloths, and tiny horses, became trapped in the tar as they wandered into the lake to drink. Today the La Brea Tar Pits are the richest source of animal fossils in all the world!

Visitors to the tar pits can see life-sized models of prehistoric animals that were trapped in the lake. The lake, by the way, is still very much a hazard. Even the air around it smells oily. Gas bubbles rise to the surface and pop—it really looks like something out of a horror movie.

In addition to the sights outside, visitors can also see fossils taken from the tar pits and colorful exhibits in the George C. Page Museum right next door.

The Famous Sign

Almost everyone has seen pictures of the white "Hollywood" sign in the hills north of Hollywood. It has become the symbol for the land of movie stars. Its huge letters were first erected in 1923, and have been replaced a few times since then.

Many people don't know that the sign was built as an advertisement for a new (in 1923) housing development in Beachwood Canyon, directly below the sign. In fact, the sign originally said "Hollywoodland"—the name of the development—but the "land" part fell off!

The letters were 30 feet wide and more than 50 feet high. Several hundred light bulbs were used to illuminate each letter. After the development proved to be a success, the sign was no longer needed. But by then people were quite attached to the sign and wanted it to stay.

Over the years, however, vandals got to it and stole all of the light bulbs. Eventually the sign deteriorated, too, and it was clear that if it was to stay as a landmark, it had to be rebuilt. In 1949, and again in 1970, the letters were replaced.

In 1978 it needed to be completely rebuilt again. To make the sign very durable, it was decided to make the letters out of metal, and to

First built in 1923, the famous Hollywood sign has since been rebuilt three times. In 1978, each letter cost $28,000.

Los Angeles International Airport is one of the busiest airports in the world.

coat them with baked enamel paint. The letters would be held fast in the ground by concrete bases. There was a little problem—each of these huge letters would cost $28,000! A few celebrities came to the rescue and donated the cost of an entire letter—among them singer Alice Cooper, Andy Williams, and Gene Autry.

The sign has also been the site of tragedies. More than one suicide has been committed from the letter "H"—the first by a young girl who had been trying unsuccessfully to become an actress.

GOVERNING THE PEOPLE

At the head of Los Angeles' city government is the mayor, who is elected for a four-year term. In addition to preparing the budget for the city, the mayor must appoint the members of Los Angeles' 23 commissions.

Each of the commissions is in

charge of one area of the city's management. For example, all the police officers are under the control of the police commission. All of the work at the Port of Los Angeles is controlled by the harbor commission. Each of the 23 commissions is responsible for choosing the head of

Los Angeles is a city of many tall palm trees—and some tall buildings, as well.

its commission. This person is called a commissioner.

In addition to the office of mayor, there is a City Council made up of 15 members. Each member is elected for a four-year term by the people in his or her district. The Los Angeles City Council is the only city council in the United States that meets Monday through Friday, every week of the year.

The relationship of the mayor and the council is a little like that of the President and Congress. The City Council is responsible for approving the budget which the mayor proposes. The Council also votes on accepting or rejecting any new ideas the mayor has. If the mayor doesn't like a law that the Council has passed, he or she can veto, or reject it. If the Council feels very strongly that the idea was a good one, however, it can vote again. If two-thirds of the Council members vote for it, it becomes law.

The city of Los Angeles has a budget of about $700 million every year. Most of that money comes from property tax, sales tax, and license fees. In 1979 the citizens of California voted on Proposition 13, which changed how that state could raise money.

Proposition 13 was a protest by people who felt that their homes were being taxed at an increasingly higher rate every year, and often the taxes were far too high for them to afford. The new law said that there was a limit to the amount of property tax. While one-third of the taxes collected from Californians used to come from property taxes, now the percentage is lower. People don't feel anymore as though they are being taxed out of their homes.

The current mayor of Los Angeles is Thomas Bradley, a black man who is extremely popular with L.A. residents. He was first elected in 1973, when he defeated Sam Yorty. Los Angeles has traditionally been a Democratic city.

FINDING A BETTER WAY

Paying the Price

Los Angeles has been called "the first truly 20th century city." This is because its layout has evolved as a result of the automobile. Other large cities depended on some sort of a mass transportation scheme, be it subways, buses, or trains. This provides cities like Boston, Chicago, or New York with a more centralized city, with the downtown area being the busiest and most important.

But L.A.'s development is more like a crazy-quilt. There are "little cities" all around the L.A. area, each with its own downtown, its own center, and its own shopping districts. Because there is no dependable mass transportation, everyone uses cars.

There is nothing really wrong about this type of city, except that it has created the need for millions and millions of cars. The cars, in turn, create all kinds of traffic jams when they meet on L.A.'s freeway system. One recent advertisement called attention to the growing traffic problem in the city. Showing a tangled web of cars and trucks, the ad said, "Once you move here you'll never move again!"

L.A. Air

Another problem with all those cars is that they create lots of exhaust. Harmful gases fill the air, and while this would be unpleasant in any city, it is downright dangerous in Los Angeles.

L.A. lies in a basin rimmed by mountains. This means that when much pollution is in the air, it's hard for breezes to clear the pollution, or smog, as it is called, from the air. The mountains keep the bad yellowish

The Harbor Freeway is one of many roads connecting the "little cities" that make up L.A.

Car exhaust and industrial pollution create smog in the Los Angeles basin. The air is trapped by surrounding mountains and can cause burning eyes and difficulty in breathing.

air trapped in the L.A. basin.

Smog kills plants, hurts eyes, and makes it hard to breathe. In L.A. there are several days every year when the smog gets so thick that the city issues an alert. This is to warn people to cut down on driving, and for L.A.'s many factories to decrease use of fuel oils.

Natural Violence

Los Angeles has long, dry summers which cause much of the brush and grasses in the hills around the city to become dry. In early fall there is always the threat of bad fires. To make matters worse, the fires are often fanned by hot strong winds from the southeast, called the Santa Anas.

Because many residents live in the hills and canyons near this dry brush, homes are frequently destroyed by fire. In 1970, for example, more than 400 homes were destroyed by fires which burned out of control for many days.

Earthquakes are another danger that residents of L.A. have learned to expect. The L.A. basin is a region particularly prone to earthquake activity.

Most of the earthquakes are pretty mild—a faint rumbling and shaking of the ground. But there have been severe quakes, such as the one in 1971 that caused the deaths of 64 people. More than $500 million dollars of property was lost in San Fernando, just north of the L.A. city limits.

Unnatural Violence

There are some types of dangers, some forms of violence that people can't control. Earthquakes and brush fires are two examples. But Los Angeles also experiences a great deal of violence that is caused not by nature, but by people. The reasons for this violence are not easy to explain, or to understand.

Because of the poverty in the city, particularly among the Chicano and black communities, many young people have turned to gangs to make themselves feel wanted. More than

At night, the Santa Monica Freeway easily moves people—and their cars—through the L.A. area. During rush hours, however, traffic on the freeways can come to a standstill.

Unstable land in the L.A. area causes many problems in the building of homes and roads.

600 gangs operate freely in the L.A. area. In fact, the city is known as "the gang capital of the United States." There are more than 70,000 members, and most of them are armed and dangerous.

In L.A., gangs control most of the "crack" and other drugs sold in their neighborhoods. They steal, they fight, and they kill. In the first four months of 1988, there were 109 gang-related killings in the L.A. area.

Many of the gangs use automatic weapons. Many have special rules for boys who want to become gang members. Sometimes a boy is asked to perform a "drive-by" killing— shooting someone at random from the back of a car. Usually the victim is unknown to the gangs. Many victims are children.

L.A. officials have tried to stay even with the gangs by employing former gang members. These people can speak the language of the gangs, and can often cool down hot tempers before violence erupts. But police in L.A. are nervous; they know that poverty, poor education, and drugs are a dangerous mixture on the streets of their city.

New Directions

Los Angeles is no different from other large cities in that it knows that to survive its problems, it needs the support and help of its people. The city is working to improve its education and job programs, so more people will be able to rise out of the poor neighborhoods. Many areas now offer free English classes for those who have language difficulties.

As L.A. approaches the 21st century, the city knows that there are still plenty of challenges it must meet. However, the pioneer spirit for which Angelenos are famous will be a strong defense against decline. As one resident smiled, "How could we fail—we're the city of the angels!"

The beauty of the area is one reason L.A. is called the "City of the Angels."

The Los Angeles area is home to seven million Angelenos who must solve many problems as the population continues to grow.

*Los Angeles, California

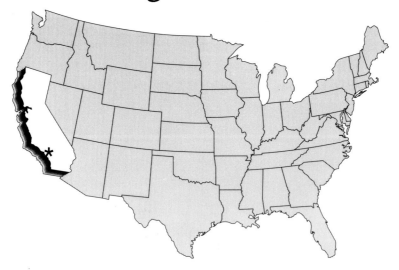

IMPORTANT FACTS

- Population: 3,361,500 (1988 estimate)
    2nd largest U.S. city
- Population of metropolitan area: 8,295,900
- Mayor: Tom Bradley (next election June
    1989)
- Seat of Los Angeles County

- Land area: 470 sq. miles
- Monthly normal temperature:
    January—56°F
    July—69°F
- Average annual precipitation: 12.08"
- Latitude: 34° 03' 15" N
- Longitude: 118° 14' 28" W
- Altitude: ranges from sea level to 5,081 ft.

- Time zone: Pacific

- Annual events:
    Easter Sunrise Services, Hollywood Bowl
    Hanamatsuri (Buddhist festival), early
      April
    Cinco de Mayo Celebration (Spanish festi-
      val), May
    Asian Cultural Festival, mid-July

IMPORTANT DATES

1500's—area of L.A. inhabited by Shoshoni
    Indians. Their village was called Yang-na.
1769—Spanish explorer Gaspar de Portola
    and priest Juan Crespi renamed Yang-na
    "Nuestra Señora la Reina de Los Angeles
    de Porciuncula."
1781—Los Angeles was founded.
1821—Mexico won its independence from
    Spain. All of California was now con-
    trolled by Mexico.
1846—Mexico lost the war with the U.S. and
    signed a treaty giving the U.S. all rights to
    California. California Gold Rush began.
1850—L.A. incorporated as a city.
1890's—oil discovered in area.
1914—Artificial harbor built near San Pedro
    Bay.
1920's—rise of motion picture and aircraft
    industries.
1965—Watts race riots left 34 dead and
    1,000 injured.
1970—fire destroyed 400 homes.
1971—earthquake killed 64 people.
mid-1980's—L.A. passed Chicago as
    nation's second largest city.

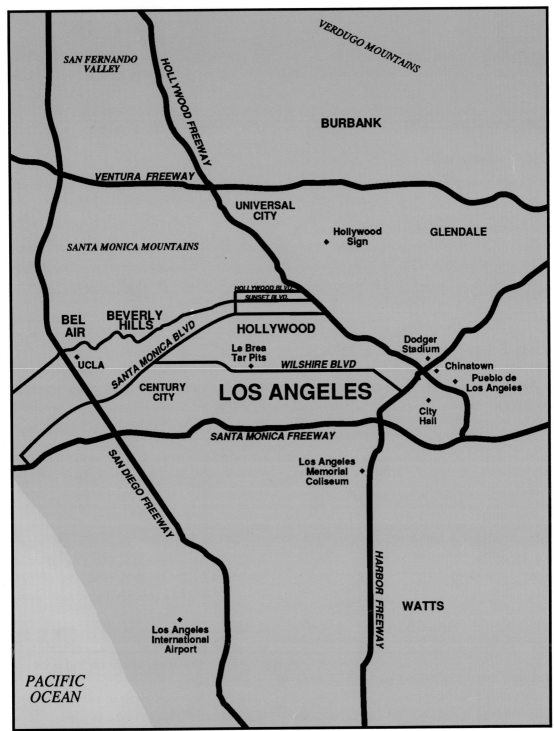

SAN FERNANDO VALLEY

VERDUGO MOUNTAINS

HOLLYWOOD FREEWAY

BURBANK

VENTURA FREEWAY

UNIVERSAL CITY

Hollywood Sign

GLENDALE

SANTA MONICA MOUNTAINS

HOLLYWOOD BLVD.
SUNSET BLVD.

BEL AIR

BEVERLY HILLS

SANTA MONICA BLVD

HOLLYWOOD

Le Brea Tar Pits

WILSHIRE BLVD.

Dodger Stadium

Chinatown
Pueblo de Los Angeles

UCLA

CENTURY CITY

LOS ANGELES

City Hall

SANTA MONICA FREEWAY

SAN DIEGO FREEWAY

Los Angeles Memorial Coliseum

HARBOR FREEWAY

WATTS

Los Angeles International Airport

PACIFIC OCEAN

©1989 Mark E. Ahlstrom

★ GLOSSARY ★

Angeleno—a resident of Los Angeles.

Barrio—Spanish for "neighborhood." The barrio in Los Angeles is the east area of the city.

Beverly Hills—an area of West L.A. noted for its beautiful and spacious homes. Many movie stars live in Beverly Hills.

Chicano—another word for a Mexican-American.

Commissioner—the head of one of L.A.'s 25 city departments.

Crespi, Juan—the priest who accompanied explorer Gaspar de Portola on his journey to Southern California in 1769.

Hollywood—an area of Central Los Angeles where most of the television and movie studios are located.

Illegal—a person who has crossed over the border of the United States without permission.

Mission—a church built by Spanish priests. There are many old missions near Los Angeles.

Nuestra Señora la Reina de Los Angeles de Porciuncula—the original name of the city of Los Angeles. It means "Our Lady Queen of the Angels of Porciuncula."

Olvera Street—the original main street of Los Angeles.

Portola, Gaspar de—the Portuguese explorer who in 1769 came to the area that is now Los Angeles.

Santa Anas—the strong southwesterly winds that blow across the mountains in the fall. The Santa Anas often make the brush fires even more dangerous.

Smith, Jebediah—the first American to journey to Los Angeles from the East.

smog—pollution in L.A. caused by a mixture of humid air from the ocean and exhaust fumes from automobiles and industry.

Sunset Boulevard—25-mile-long street that winds its way from the downtown area to the Pacific coast.

veto—to reject.

Walk of Fame—the area along Hollywood Boulevard decorated with 2,500 stars, each with the name of a famous movie star.

Watts—an area of South Central Los Angeles which was the site of rioting in 1965. Most of the residents of Watts are black and poor.

Yang-na—Shoshoni village of the 1500's. Now the site of modern Los Angeles.